SHEDDING A SKIN

by AMANDA WILKIN

Shedding a Skin was first performed on 17 June 2021 at
Soho Theatre, London, and live-streamed on 15 July 2021

Soho Theatre presents

SHEDDING A SKIN
by AMANDA WILKIN

Writer and Performer	Amanda Wilkin
Director	Elayce Ismail
Set and Costume Designer	Rosanna Vize
Lighting Designer	Jess Bernberg
Projection Designer	Nina Dunn
Sound Designer and Composer	Richard Hammarton
Dramaturg	Gillian Greer
Assistant Director	Nimmo Ismail
Production Manager	Seb Cannings
Stage Manager	Rachael Head
Assistant Stage Manager	Lauren Taylor
Costume Supervisor	Megan Rarity
Marketing	SINE Digital
PR	Fourth Wall PR
Production Photography	Helen Murray
Producer	Ameena Hamid

Sponsored by NJA Ltd
Creative Management

WINNER:
VERITY BARGATE
AWARD 2020
sponsored by

CAST AND CREATIVE TEAM

AMANDA WILKIN | WRITER AND PERFORMER

Amanda is a playwright, actress and jazz and blues singer-songwriter from London. In 2017 she was on the Royal Court and BBC London Writers' Groups and her first play AND I DREAMT I WAS DROWNING was developed as part of the Talawa Firsts Festival in 2018. She has since written and performed short pieces at the Sam Wanamaker Playhouse, THE LITTLE SOB as part of Dark Night of the Soul in early 2019, and BESSIE COLEMAN about the first African American female pilot as part of Notes to the Forgotten She-Wolves in early 2020. She is under commission to Audible as part of their Emerging Playwrights Programme 2020 and to Headlong Theatre Company, where she is also Writer in Residence 2021/22. She is also part of the Young Women Opera Makers Aix-en Provence's Opera residency 2021/22. Recent work includes the audio play RECOGNITION about the C19th's famous mixed race composer Samuel Coleridge-Taylor for 45North Ltd/Ellie Keel Productions (released 2021).

As an actor, Amanda's theatre credits include: EMILIA (Shakespeare's Globe & West End); WHITE TEETH (Kiln Theatre); GRINNING MAN (Trafalgar Studios); THE 306:DAY (National Theatre Scotland); LA RONDE (The Bunker Theatre); PILGRIMS (Theatre Clwyd/HighTide Festival/The Yard Theatre); HAMLET (tour to every country in the world), A MIDSUMMER NIGHT'S DREAM, GABRIEL, THE TEMPEST (Shakespeare's Globe); HOPELESSLY DEVOTED (Paines Plough & Birmingham REP); ARABIAN NIGHTS (Watermill Theatre); THE BACCHAE, BLOOD WEDDING (Royal and Derngate); MARAT/SADE, A MIDSUMMER NIGHT'S DREAM (RSC); STAMPING, SHOUTING AND SINGING HOME (Nuffield Theatre) and THE TWITS (Dukes Theatre).

Television includes: FINDING ALICE (ITV); UNFORGOTTEN (ITV); GIRLFRIEND EXPERIENCE (STARZ); HOLBY CITY (BBC1); BERLIN STATION (EPIX); DOCTORS (BBC1) and GAVIN AND STACEY (BBC3 & Baby Cow Productions).

Film includes: MAMMA MIA: HERE WE GO AGAIN! (Obscure Pictures).

Amanda trained at Royal Welsh College of Music & Drama.

ELAYCE ISMAIL | DIRECTOR

Elayce Ismail is a director and dramaturg, working in the UK and internationally across theatre, opera and film. She is the Artistic Associate at Music Theatre Wales and has previously been the Head of New Work at the Donmar Warehouse; the inaugural RTYDS Associate Director at Northern Stage; and a Resident Director at the National Theatre as the recipient of the JP Morgan Award for Emerging Directors.

Theatre direction includes: NANJING (Shakespeare's Globe); IF NOT NOW, WHEN? (National Theatre); UNDER MILK WOOD, THE WAR OF THE WORLDS (Northern Stage); GIRLS (Soho Theatre/HighTide Festival/British Council Edinburgh Showcase); THE RISE AND SHINE OF COMRADE FIASCO, CHORUS, SPOOKY ACTION AT A DISTANCE (Gate); THE LOST RING (Deutsches Theater Berlin); STAY ANOTHER SONG (Young Vic).

Opera includes: OUR DARK SIDE AND THE MOON (creator/librettist; Royal Opera House); THEY WHISPER DON'T GAZE AT THE STARS… (director; ENO); 4:48 PSYCHOSIS (revival director; Opéra national du Rhin/Royal Opera House); A MIDSUMMER NIGHT'S DREAM (associate director; Opéra Orchestre national Montpellier); THE VIRTUES OF THINGS (assistant director; Royal Opera House).

Film includes: NANJING (director; Theatertreffen Stückemarkt); AMAZON (creator/writer; MTW/London Sinfonietta); SIMONE (director; Young Vic).

ROSANNA VIZE | SET AND COSTUME DESIGNER

Forthcoming credits include: MAVRA AND PIERROT LUNAIRE (Royal Opera House, Covent Garden), GULLIVERS TRAVELS (Unicorn Theatre); THE TWO CHARACTER PLAY (Hampstead Theatre, Upstairs); GLASS MENAGERIE (Royal Exchange, Manchester), CAT ON A HOT TIN ROOF (Curve Theatre and UK Tour), THE ENEMY (Royal National Theatre of Scotland).

Theatre credits include: HARM (Bush Theatre), THE COMEBACK (Sonia Friedman Productions, Noel Coward theatre – West End), HARM FILM (BBC Films), INCANTATA (Irish Rep Theatre, NYC), HEDDA GABLER (Sherman Theatre); THE PHLEBOTOMIST (Hampstead Theatre, Upstairs); MIDSUMMER PARTY (The Old Vic); THE AUDIENCE (Nuffield Theatre, Southampton);DON CARLOS (Exeter Northcott); INCANTATA (Galway Festival); AN ADVENTURE, LEAVE TAKING (The Bush Theatre); YOUS TWO (Hampstead Theatre); THE ALMIGHTY SOMETIMES (Royal Exchange Theatre); KING LEAR (Globe Theatre); EARTHWORKS AND MYTH (RSC); LOW LEVEL PANIC (Orange Tree Theatre); AFTER OCTOBER (Finborough Theatre); HENRY I (Reading Between the Lines); GIRLS (Soho Theatre, Hightide & Talawa Theatre); FUP AND NOYE'S FLUDDE (Kneehigh Theatre); DARK LAND LIGHTHOUSE (Bristol Old Vic); ST JOAN OF THE STOCKYARDS (Bristol Old Vic); A THOUSAND SEASONS PASSED (Bristol Old Vic); THE TINDER BOX (Bristol Old Vic); THE LAST DAYS OF MANKIND (Bristol Old Vic); TALON (Bristol Old Vic); DIARY OF A MADMAN (The Gate Theatre); THE RISE AND SHINE OF COMRADE FIASCO (The Gate Theatre); Infinite Lives (Tobacco Factory Theatre); BANKSY: THE ROOM IN THE ELEPHANT (Tobacco Factory Theatre and Traverse Theatre); COASTAL DEFENCES (Tobacco Factory Theatre).

JESS BERNBERG | LIGHTING DESIGNER

Jess trained at Guildhall School of Music and Drama and was the 2018 Laboratory Associate Lighting Designer at Nuffield Southampton Theatres.

Designs include: [BLANK] (Donmar Warehouse); OVERFLOW, RUST, AND THE REST OF ME FLOATS (Bush Theatre); THE LANGUAGE OF KINDNESS (Shoreditch Town Hall/UK Tour); SHOPPING MALLS IN TEHRAN (Traverse/Home Manchester/BAC); ACTUALLY (Trafalgar Studios 2); OUT OF WATER, COUGAR (Orange Tree Theatre); WE ANCHOR IN HOPE, DEVIL WITH THE BLUE DRESS, FCUK'D (Off West End Award nomination) (The Bunker); THE CRUCIBLE, SEX SEX MEN MEN, A NEW AND BETTER YOU,

BUGGY BABY (The Yard); DICK WHITTINGTON (Theatre Royal Stratford East); OTHELLO (Cambridge Arts Theatre); WONDROUS VULVA (Oval House); THE TOWN THAT TREES BUILT (Young Vic); AND THE REST OF ME FLOATS(Birmingham Rep/Bush Theatre); THE BORROWERS (Tobacco Factory); VICTORIA'S KNICKERS, CONSENSUAL (NYT); MEDUSA, MUCH ADO ABOUT NOTHING, DUNGENESS, LOVE AND INFORMATION (Nuffield Southampton Theatres); HOMOS, OR EVERYONE IN AMERICA (Finborough Theatre); SONGLINES (HighTide).

Awards: 2017 Association of Lighting Designer's Francis Reid Award

NINA DUNN | PROJECTION DESIGNER

Nina has designed Video & Projections for a wide range of shows, working internationally and spanning Theatre, Opera, Dance, Musical Theatre, Immersive, Fashion, Opening Ceremonies and Live Events and Public Art. She is also an educator within her industry, helping to devise and deliver undergraduate courses and mentoring programs in leading UK institutions.

Theatre includes CITY OF ANGELS (West End); 9 TO 5 THE MUSICAL (West End / UK Tour); CINDERELLA (Imagine Theatre); A MUSEUM IN BAGHDAD, VENICE PRESERVED, Miss Littlewood, THE SEVEN ACTS OF MERCY, VOLPONE (RSC); PLENTY, COPENHAGEN, FIDDLER ON THE ROOF, FORTY YEARS ON (Chichester Festival Theatre), CBEEBIES HANSEL AND GRETEL (BBC); GOING THROUGH (Bush Theatre); COOKIES (Theatre Royal Haymarket); THE MOUNTAINTOP (Young Vic, UK Tour); NO MAN'S LAND (Tour/West End); ALICE'S ADVENTURES UNDERGROUND (London / China); THE ASSASSINATION OF KATIE HOPKINS (Theatr Clwyd), THE BOX OF DELIGHTS (Wilton's Music Hall); DER FREISCHÜTZ, MACBETH (Wiener Staatsoper); SPRING GALA (Royal Opera House);THE LIFE, THE DIARY OF A TEENAGE GIRL, USAGI YOJIMBO (Southwark Playhouse); THE DAMNED UNITED (West Yorkshire Playhouse / Tour); THE HOOK, ALONE IN BERLIN (Royal & Derngate); PHANTOM OF THE OPERA (Cameron Mackintosh, UK/US/Australia Tour); THE FLYING DUTCHMAN (ENO); LA TRAVIATA, HIPPOLYTE ET ARICIE (Glyndebourne); EMPEROR AND GALILEAN (National Theatre), THE ROCKY HORROR SHOW (European Tour)

RICHARD HAMMARTON | SOUND DESIGNER & COMPOSER

Theatre credits include: DEATH OF A BLACK MAN (Hampstead); SHOOK (Southwark Playhouse/ Trafalgar studios); VALUED FRIENDS (Rose Theatre, Kingston); CHIAROSCURO (Bush Theatre); RED DUST ROAD (National Theatre Scotland); GHOSTS (Royal and Derngate, Northampton); WOLFIE (Theatre503); PRINCESS AND THE HUSTLER (Eclipse Theatre Company); LOST PARADISE (New Visual Paradigm); UNDER MILKWOOD (Northern Stage); WOMEN IN POWER (Nuffield Theatre); DESCRIBE THE NIGHT (Hampstead Theatre); LOVE FROM A STRANGER (Royal & Derngate, Northampton); HANNA (Papatango); IN THE EVENT OF MOONE DISASTER (Theatre503); TRESTLE (Papatango); BURNING DOORS (Belarus Free Theatre); GIRLS (HighTide); THE WEIR (English Touring Theatre); DEPOSIT

(Hampstead Theatre); AS YOU LIKE IT (Theatre by the Lake); FAUST X2 (The Watermill Theatre); DIRTY GREAT LOVE STORY (Arts Theatre); ASSATA TAUGHT ME (Gate Theatre); LOW LEVEL PANIC (Orange Tree Theatre); ORCA (Papatango); LUV (Park Theatre); MUCH ADO ABOUT NOTHING, JUMPY (Theatr Clwyd); LINDA (Royal Court); THE CRUCIBLE (Manchester Royal Exchange); COMRADE FIASCO (Gate Theatre); A NUMBER (Nuffield Theatre/Young Vic); GRIMM TALES 2 (Bargehouse, Oxo Tower Wharf); GHOST FROM A PERFECT PLACE (Arcola); THE CRUCIBLE (Old Vic); DEALER'S CHOICE (Royal & Derngate, Northampton); SIZWE BANSI IS DEAD (Theatre Royal Stratford East & UK tour); KINGSTON 14 (Theatre Royal Stratford East); BRILLIANT ADVENTURES (Manchester Royal Exchange);; DR FAUSTUS (Manchester Royal Exchange - Winner of MEN Best Design Award); THE PITCHFORK DISNEY (Arcola); EDWARD II (Manchester Royal Exchange); SIX CHARACTERS LOOKING FOR AN AUTHOR (Young Vic);

Television credits include: RIPPER STREET, NO WIN NO FEE, SEX 'N' DEATH, WIPEOUT, THE SHIP (BBC); AGATHA CHRISTIE'S MARPLE (ITV);

Radio credits include: THE EFFECT (BBC Radio 3).

Orchestration work: AGATHA CHRISTIE'S MARPLE SERIES 1 & 2, PRIMEVAL, JERICHO, IF I HAD YOU (ITV); DRACULA, A HISTORY OF BRITAIN, SILENT WITNESS, DALZIEL AND PASCOE (BBC); ALICE THROUGH THE LOOKING GLASS (Channel 4); THE NINE LIVES OF TOMAS KATZ AND SCENES OF A SEXUAL NATURE (feature films, UK).

NIMMO ISMAIL | ASSISTANT DIRECTOR

Nimmo Ismail is a theatre director and writer living in London.

Theatre work as a director includes GLEE & ME by Stuart Slade, THE CHRISTMAS STAR by Russell T Davies (both Royal Exchange Manchester), FRAGMENTS by Cordelia Lynn as part of Five Plays and MY ENGLAND by Somalia Seaton as part of Fresh Direction (both at Young Vic) SNAP by Danusia Samal as part of Connect Now (Old Vic), TWO PALESTINIANS GO DOGGING by Sami Ibrahim (Sparkhaus Theatre), THE OTHER DAY; TWELVE MONTHS' NOTICE; THE DEBATE and WINTER BLOSSOM KARAOKE by Leaphia Darko (Camden People's Theatre); TELEVISION GUIDE by Brad Birch; THE DISPLACED/WE CAME IN A TINY RED BOAT by Jerusha Green and I ACTUALLY HAVE A SON by Andrew Maddock (all Guildhall School of Music & Drama with Squint Theatre).

Theatre work as a writer includes THREE DATES (Southwark Playhouse), NEW WAYS OF LOOKING (Bush Theatre) and HATCH (Talawa Theatre Company)

She took part in the Royal Court Writers Programme, Talawa Theatre Company's TYPT, Bush Theatre's 2020/2021 Allotments Programme and is a member of the Orange Tree Writers Collective 2021/2022.

Theatre work as a staff/assistant director includes THE ANTIPODES by Annie Baker (National Theatre) OUR TOWN by Thorton Wilder (Open Air Theatre) A VERY VERY VERY DARK MATTER by Martin McDonagh (Bridge Theatre), THE PRUDES by Anthony Neilson and GOATS by Liwaa Yazji (both Royal Court);

WINGS by Arthur Kopit (Young Vic) THE PHLEBOTOMIST by Ella Road (Hampstead Theatre) and QUARTER LIFE CRISIS by Yolanda Mercy (Brixton House and Edinburgh Fringe).

RACHAEL HEAD | STAGE MANAGER

Rachael is a Stage Manager with a background in Production. She first became interested in Theatre during her Literature degree and started her own Theatre Company in 2015. After two years Rachael moved into Stage Management and her SM credits include RUN SISTER RUN (Sheffield Theatres), TAMING OF THE SHREW (The Globe Theatre), WHITEWASH (Soho Theatre), SQUARE GO and cover on BABY REINDEER & DO OUR BEST (Francesca Moody Productions), and THE ARTIST (Circo Aereo).

Rachael is also Radio Producer for BBC Wales and the Podcast Producer at DASH Arts.

LAUREN TAYLOR | ASSISTANT STAGE MANAGER

Lauren Taylor is a London-born Stage Manager who trained at the Royal Academy of Dramatic Art.

Her theatre credits include HARRY POTTER AND THE CURSED CHILD (Sonia Friedman Productions), SON OF THE NILE (Utopia Theatre), EVERYTHING MUST GO (These Girls), BEYOND THE CANON (2019), and THE AMERICAN CLOCK (The Old Vic).

MEGAN RARITY | COSTUME SUPERVISOR

Megan trained at Arts University Bournemouth in Costume for Performance Design.

Credits include: GARSINGTON OPERA FESTIVAL 2021 (Wormsley Estate); THE COMEBACK (Noël Coward Theatre); LITTLE SHOP OF HORRORS (LAMDA); CINDERELLA THE MUSICAL (Nuffield Southampton Theatre); HEDDA GABLER (Sherman Theatre); SHOOK (Southwark Playhouse/UK tour); VALUED FRIENDS (Rose Theatre Kingston), MIDSUMMER NIGHTS PARTY (The Old Vic); THE AUDIENCE (Nuffield Southampton Theatre); BLOOD KNOT (Orange Tree Theatre); WEST SIDE STORY (Hartshorn-Hook Productions); EDEN (Hampstead Theatre); UBU KARAOKE (Kneehigh Theatre Company); UTILITY (Orange Tree Theatre); MAYFLY (Orange Tree Theatre); A STREETCAR NAMED DESIRE (Nuffield Southampton Theatre); EUGENIUS! (The Other Palace); BEAUTY AND THE BEAST (Watersmeet Theatre); TRYST (Tabard Theatre); INSIGNIFICANCE (The Arcola); ZIGGER ZAGGER (National Youth Theatre); DIRECTORS FESTIVAL SEASON: MISTERMAN, END OF HOPE, ALBERT'S BOY, EVEN STILLNESS BREATHES SLOWLY AGAINST A BRICK WALL, WASTED (The Orange Tree Theatre); OKLAHOMA! (Bennet Memorial Diocesan School); POSH (Pleasance Theatre); THE TEMPEST (The Print Room).

AMEENA HAMID | PRODUCER

Ameena is a London based creative producer, general manager, festival curator and facilitator. Her work focuses on increasing inclusivity and representation in theatre. She has been heralded as 'a true role model to the future generations' by Official London Theatre. Ameena was an EdFringe and British Council Emerging Producer and one of Stage One's Bridge the Gap Producers. She is on the Board of the League of Independent Producers and part of the Creative Freelances Shaping London's Recovery Advisory Group. At just 20, Ameena earnt the accolade of youngest ever female producer on the West End as Associate Producer on DEATH DROP (Garrick Theatre).

Other credits include: Co-Producer THE WIZ (Hope Mill Theatre Manchester), General Manager on WONDERMENT MAGIC AND ILLUSION (Palace Theatre), Assistant Producer to THE SHOW MUST GO ON LIVE (Palace Theatre), Producer on GRADUATES AT CADOGAN HALL, Producer on EATING MYSELF (Applecart Arts and FAE Lima, Peru), Producer on KILLING IT and SINCE U BEEN GONE (VAULT Festival)

Soho Theatre is London's most vibrant producer for new theatre, comedy and cabaret. We pursue creative excellence, harnessing an artistic spirit that is based in our new writing roots, the radical ethos of the fringe and the traditions of punk culture and queer performance. We champion voices that challenge from outside of the mainstream, and sometimes from within it too. We value entertainment, accessibility and enjoy a good show. We are a registered charity and social enterprise and our audiences are diverse in age, background and outlook.

We are mission driven and we measure our success in:
- the NEW WORK that we produce, present and facilitate
- the CREATIVE TALENT that we nurture with artists, in our participation work and with our own staff
- the DIVERSE AUDIENCES that we play to and engage

To create theatre we nurture new playwrights, we commission new work and we produce new plays. Writers including debbie tucker green, Chris Chibnall, Theresa Ikoko and Vicky Jones had early work produced at Soho. With comedy and cabaret, we identify, develop and produce exciting new talents and present some of the biggest international stars.

We work beyond Soho taking work to and from the world's major festivals like the Edinburgh Festival Fringe. Our touring work plays across the UK and internationally with strong connections to India, Australia and the US. Our filmed comedy can be downloaded on our digital platform, seen on TV and viewed on international airlines. We're ambitious, entrepreneurial and collaborative and take pride in our strong relationships with commercial partners – but the profits we make go back into supporting our work.

sohotheatre.com | www.sohotheatreondemand.com | @sohotheatre

THE VERITY BARGATE AWARD

For 50 years Soho Theatre has championed new writing, from lunch time plays in the 70s to today's commissions, attachments, writers labs and awards. Since 1982, Soho Theatre's prestigious biennial playwriting competition, the Verity Bargate Award, has uncovered the best new play by an emerging UK and Irish writer and launched the careers of some of Britain's most established writers. The winning play receiving a cash prize and produced in a full production on our stages. The Award honours **Verity Bargate**, Soho's co-founder who passionately championed new writing during her time at the small but hugely influential fringe theatre, Soho Poly.

On the search for extraordinary plays from extraordinary voices, the Verity Bargate Award 2020, sponsored by Character 7, received almost 1500 new plays by emerging writers. The Award was chaired by film and television producer Character 7's Stephen Garrett (*The Undoing*) with a judging panel of industry experts including Lolita Chakrabati (*Hymn*), Russell T Davies (*It's a Sin*), Laura Wade (*The Watsons*) and Phoebe Waller-Bridge (*Fleabag*). Amanda Wilkin's spellbinding play *Shedding a Skin* captivated the Award's readers and judges and has now been produced by Soho Theatre in a production sponsored by NJA, Core Values & Creative Management, from 17 June to 17 July 2001.

For more information on the Verity Bargate Award and other ways writers can connect with Soho Theatre – including workshops, lab programmes, readings, notes sessions, and script submissions – please visit **www.sohotheatre.com/writers**

SUPPORTERS

Principal Supporters
Nicholas Allott OBE
Hani Farsi
Hedley and Fiona Goldberg
Michael and Isobel Holland
Jack and Linda Keenan
Amelia and Neil Mendoza
Lady Susie Sainsbury
Carolyn Ward
Jennifer and Roger Wingate

Supporting Partners
Matthew Bunting
Denzil Fernandez
Stephen Garrett
Beatrice Hollond
Angela Hyde-Courtney
Phil & Jane Radcliff
Dom & Ali Wallis
Garry Watts

Corporate Supporters
Adnams Southwold
Bargate Murray
Bates Wells & Braithwaite
Cameron Mackintosh Ltd
Character Seven
EPIC Private Equity
Financial Express
Fosters
The Groucho Club
John Lewis Oxford Street
Latham & Watkins LLP
Lionsgate UK
NJA
The Nadler Hotel
Oberon Books Ltd
Overbury Leisure
Quo Vardis
Richmond Associates
Soho Estates
Soundcraft

Trusts & Foundations
The 29th May 1961 Charitable Trust
The Andor Charitable Trust
Backstage Trust
Bruce Wake Charitable Trust
The Boris Karloff Charitable Foundation
The Boshier-Hinton Foundation
The Buzzacott Stuart Defries Memorial Fund
Chapman Charitable Trust
The Charles Rifkind and Jonathan Levy Charitable Settlement
The Charlotte Bonham-Carter Charitable Trust
Cockayne – Grants for the Arts and The London Community Foundation
John S Cohen Foundation
The David and Elaine Potter Foundation
The D'Oyly Carte Charitable Trust
The Eranda Rothschild Foundation
The Ernest Cook Trust
Esmée Fairbairn Foundation
The Fenton Arts Trust
Fidelio Charitable Trust
Foyle Foundation
Garrick Charitable Trust
The Goldsmiths' Company
The Late Mrs Margaret Guido's Charitable Trust
Harold Hyam Wingate Foundation
Hyde Park Place Estate Charity
The Ian Mactaggart Trust
The Idlewild Trust
The John Thaw Foundation
John Ellerman Foundation
John Lewis Oxford Street Community Matters Scheme
John Lyon's Charity
JP Getty Jnr Charitable Trust
The Kobler Trust
Lara Atkin Charitable Foundation
The Leche Trust
The Mackintosh Foundation
Mohamed S. Farsi Foundation
Noel Coward Foundation
The Peggy Ramsay Foundation
The Prudence Trust
The Rose Foundation
The Royal Victoria Hall Foundation
Santander Foundation
Schroder Charity Trust
St Giles-in-the-Fields and William Shelton Educational Charity
The St James's Piccadilly Charity
Tallow Chandlers Benevolent Fund
The Teale Charitable Trust
The Theatres Trust
The Thistle Trust
Unity Theatre Charitable Trust
The Wolfson Foundation

Soho Theatre Performance Friends
Dave Barnett
Rajan Brotia
Alban Gordon
Andrew Lucas
Walter Ken McCracken and Stacie Styles
Gary Wilder

Soho Theatre Playwright Friends
David Aukin
John Bannister
Quentin Bargate
Tim Crocker-Buque
Emily Fletcher
Liam Goddard
Fawn James
John James
Shappi Khorsandi
Jeremy King OBE
Lesley Symons
Henry Wyndham
Christopher Yu

Soho Theatre Comedy Friends
Oladipo Agboluaje
Stephen Allan
Fran Allen
Katherine Andreen
Samantha Arnold
James Atkinson
Polly Balsom
Ronald Balzan
Uri Baruchin
Antonio Batista
David Baynard
Kieran Birt
Matthew Boyle
Matthew Bradfield
Christian Braeker
Jesse Buckle
Oscar Cainer
Indigo Carnie
Chris Carter
Paul Cater
Lucy Collins
Haralambos Dayantis
Penelope Deans
Jeff Dormer
Peter Dudas
Edwina Ellis
Alice Evans
Stephen Ferns
Stephen Fowler
John Fry
Mathieu Gaillemin
Cyrus Gilbert-Rolfe
Cindy Glenn
Terry Good
Louise Goodman
Steven Greenwood
Paul Hardie
Anthony Hawser
Paul Hill
Karen Howlett
John Ireland
Mick Jewell
Bethan Jones
Simon Jones
Sue Jones
Jen Kavanagh
Matt Kempen
Andreas Kubat
Emily Kyne
Ian Livingston
Alejandra Lozada
Lucy MacCarthy
Julia MacMillan
Anthony Marraccino
Nicola Martin
Corrie McGuire
Kosten Metreweli
Rebecca Morgan
Nathan Mosher
Caroline Moyes
Mr and Mrs Roger Myddelton
James Nicoll
Emma Norman
Sam Owen
Alan Pardoe
Helen Pegrum
Andrew Perkins
Keith Petts
Fran Plagge
Nick Pontt
Giovanna Ramazzina
Rachel Read
Charlotte Richardson
Annabel Ridley
Antonia Rolph
Laura Ross
Tamanna Ruparel
Sabrina Russow
Natalia Siabkin
Beth Silver
Sara Simpson
Michelle Singer
Heather Smith
Hari Sriskantha
Sarah Stanford
Tracey Tattersall
Sarah Taylor
Victoria Thomas
Neil Tymlin
Gabriel Vogt
Sam Webster
Mike Welsh
David Whitehead
Matt Whitehurst
Gareth Williams
Allan Willis
Geoff Wytcherley
Liz Young
Sherry Zhou
Ben Zola

We would also like to thank those supporters who wish to remain anonymous.

We are also supported by Westminster City Council West End Ward Budget and the London Borough of Waltham Forest.

Shedding a Skin

Amanda Wilkin is a playwright, actress and jazz and blues singer-songwriter from London. In 2017 she was on the Royal Court and BBC London Writers' Groups, and her first play, *And I Dreamt I was Drowning*, was developed as part of the Talawa Firsts Festival in 2018. She has since written and performed short pieces at the Sam Wanamaker Playhouse: *The Little Sob*, as part of Dark Night of the Soul in early 2019, and *Bessie Coleman*, about the first African American female pilot, as part of Notes to the Forgotten She-Wolves in early 2020. She is under commission to Audible as part of their Emerging Playwrights Programme 2020 and to Headlong Theatre Company, where she is also Writer in Residence 2021/22. She is also part of the Young Women Opera Makers Aix-en Provence's Opera residency 2021/22. Recent work includes the audio play *Recognition* about the nineteenth century's famous mixed-race composer Samuel Coleridge-Taylor for 45 North Ltd/Ellie Keel Productions (released 2021).

AMANDA WILKIN

Shedding a Skin

faber

First published in 2021
by Faber and Faber Limited
74–77 Great Russell Street
London WC1B 3DA

Typeset by Brighton Gray
Printed and bound in the UK by CPI Group (Ltd), Croydon CR0 4YY

A CIP record for this book
is available from the British Library

978-0-571-37273-7

4 6 8 10 9 7 5

Thanks

I don't have enough words for the people who have supported me during my journey of writing this play. You are in abundance. I am so grateful.

Thank you especially
To all at Soho Theatre, the Verity Bargate Award and Faber & Faber
Our creative team, Gill, Rachael, Lauren, Nimmo and Elayce
My Welsh College gang
Olly, Morgan, Michele, Charlie, Nadia, Cheryl and Helen
Jude and Chris
Imogen

For all in my community who have held and encouraged me
For my sisters, for all the aunties
For my family
For Mum

Shedding a Skin was first performed at Soho Theatre, London, on 17 June 2021, with the following cast and creative team:

Myah Amanda Wilkin

Director Elayce Ismail
Set and Costume Designer Rosanna Vize
Lighting Designer Jess Bernberg
Projection Designer Nina Dunn
Sound Designer and Composer Richard Hammarton
Dramaturg Gillian Greer
Assistant Director Nimmo Ismail
Production Manager Seb Cannings
Stage Manager Rachael Head
Assistant Stage Manager Lauren Taylor
Costume Supervisor Megan Rarity
Marketing SINE Digital
PR Fourth Wall PR
Production Photography Helen Murray
Producer Ameena Hamid

Characters

Myah

SHEDDING A SKIN

Note

Words in italic indicate speech

**Words in bold operate in a different space
to the rest of the play
A moment of connection, somewhere else**

PROLOGUE

I would rather be anywhere. Anywhere else in the world,
right now. Than right here.

I get to the office before everyone else, for the quiet

and wonder which country the cleaner's from, but never ask

just a small

morning

and then I hunt furiously for the mug I brought in on my
first day with my

name on it

I love that mug

It's my mug

and no one else here shares my name (Myah) so I get
annoyed when

I find it about once a fortnight in the sink

old sticky furry teabag equipped inside

really?!

I wash it out, swear never to leave it in the dishwasher
again

and then I type.

There are many desks to my right, and to my left

the office fills up, with

women who munch on leaves at lunch and guys who make shit jokes

you can smell the privilege in this room

it's gross

the carpet's two shades of hideous grey

someone is always taking their daily crap in one of the two toilet cubicles

and no one really talks to each other, outside of their clique

my clique's still made of me, six months into this job

but I've somehow joined them in trying to perfect the

concentrated *we can do better* faces.

I fantasise about leaving

hourly.

I'm being asked into a conference room upstairs

not quite off my lunch break – and that's obvious, because I'm holding my Tupperware, but

umm, yeah sure, okay

and as I climb the stairs

get in the room

my head of department welcomes me

Hey! Great!! Yes, let's begin!

weird

didn't think he knew who I was – he's never properly spoken to me before

and, whoa

behind him is a huge camera

and

as I shuffle in

I look around the room to see they've rounded up all three of the total

Black and Brown faces that work in the building

too.

they're all staring at me

this is weird (am I in trouble?) what's this about?

and I'm focusing in on my supervisor

inclusivity in the workplace

blah blah

head office needs photos to back up statistics.

oh.

I feel so uncomfortable.

and look to the others to laugh, because

'diversity' in this office is not on the agenda

there was a formal complaint last month about the type of food I was

heating in the microwave, and

I've lost count of the amount of times people have

asked me about my hair

tried to touch my hair

and even

grumbled about positive quotas

in front of me!

so this feels

fake

but, in this moment

I feel pressure

and I don't know how to articulate – how to say – well how am I gonna get out of this?

as I'm herded to sit down with the others, which I do, very, very slowly

I sit

and . . . a nod between us

Black person nod

ain't done this in a while

a recognition of

it's us here – to the others sat beside me

us here

and then I notice that the person I've not met before is the cleaner – who's not in his teal uniform but instead, he's in a suit – made to look like one of us?

to bump up the numbers?!

I stop – nope

I'm on my feet, I'm up, the others look at me

I have a . . . a report thing, that I'm

(I am yelling at myself inside for being so inarticulate)

ah no problem, it can wait! Don't you worry about it – haha blame me if anyone asks so then

I nod

put back on my pleasant face, sit

– well

they're making an effort, I guess?

or . . .

I'm not listening properly

I'm quietening voices inside myself simultaneously asking
why is this such a problem and screaming *sellout!*

while

I'm smiling as the room flashes with light

I blink every time from the force

wow they're really going to town on this shoot

and my supervisor is laughing

this is great, guys . . . but look like you're having fun!

I've never felt more uncomfortable on the inside and smiley
on the out

and they wouldn't know, would they? – couldn't,

just get through it, just smile for the

stupid picture, just

get on with it already, and

smile, just

he's sipping his tea and crumbs of biscuit are falling from
the corners of his mouth –

it'll be done in a sec

he's gross

It'll be done and then you can get out of here and stop judging why you're so damn

uncomfortable all the time

and

the others are fine with it so why aren't you?

and

he's really gross

and

SMILE

and

how long left?! –

and

and he's drinking from my mug.

My mug.

My mug with my name on it.

I spring up

the others look at me, again

something has

clicked

step too far, and

What the fuck is this shoot for?

I say it louder than I thought it would come out – it just came out it just

erupted.

there's silence.

biscuit bossman can't believe I've sworn

he's turned red

and I realise I've made a tit out of myself

but I can't stop

Fucking diversity photo?! Are you insane? You don't give a shit about 'diversity'!

whoa.

I hear a tut

cameraman shifts towards me, he's huge, he pipes up

erm, no need to be so angry . . . it's just for

did he really just call me angry? did he really just use that word did he really just do

and before he finishes his sentence I've strided up to him and punched him in his eyeball and knocked him out

Bam!

yaaaaowwwwww that really, really hurt think I've broken my knuckle or something

What the hell!

is all I hear as I am a hot sweet mess and I've seen red, overcome first with rage, then with shame

I'm possessed, with a hand that really frikkin kills so

next I grab the camera and throw it on the floor

screams heard

it smashes – teeny bits of it have splintered, flown to the corners of the room

as the biscuit supervisor yells

security!

Ha. Like they'll be able to hear you from up in here

the others have sped out the room,

as I pace about

I can't stop myself

too late

but I'm not quite finished, not yet

I take a sharpie from the table and I'm scribbling in huge capitals on the wall

You're

All

Fake.

Cunts.

wish I'd thought of something more articulate!

and lastly (and most importantly) I grab my mug and stroll downstairs to my desk

a slight skip here and there

while biscuit man follows me from a distance still yelling

You can't. Treat people like this!

Everyone was watching.

It felt good as I gathered my bits, and photos, and laptop (and put laptop back because I remembered it wasn't mine) and my plant and walked to the door

I was leaving this place

most definitely sacked

obviously

and on the way out I passed the cleaner by the door

lifted my hand ready to engage in high five glory

when

I asked to be in the photograph

he said

I heard about it and I asked to be in it

I've worked here seventeen years

I wanted to feel a part of this place

my face crunched

cardboard box felt heavy

forehead hot

I took the stairs down to the ground floor rather than the lift

I walked out the main entrance and

It was raining.

You'll never be able to stand

on your own two feet

my dad said

If you keep coming back, asking for money

I answer *London is so expensive*

and yes I had to walk out of my job because it made me miserable

(I obviously didn't tell them)

and my relationship has just ended, on top of everything else

so the triad of work, love and home is really on fire right now.

what are you going to do with your life Mom says and

temperature rises

and I get it – they're just worried about me, I get it

but

I've reverted back into the child I once was complete with my oddities

and as I sink upstairs into my old room

complete with bunkbed and my revered Skunk Anansie posters

my face feels hot

throat is hoarse from that argument

but at least it's only this weekend – one weekend that I have
to reckon with this

parental hurricane and the shame.

I needed to remember that weekend fully as I climbed the
fifteen floors in a new

borough

lift's not working

fifteen floors that remind me that in the event of the zombie
apocalypse I'm

not going to survive

not going to be able to get through twenty-four hours if I
can't even make it to the

fifteenth floor

and finally

I find the door

it's not my door

not the blue hatch thing that I lived in with my now ex

the mother of all exes

the baroque-loving, climate-campaigning ex

and I loved those bits

but

the ex who had questionable opinions on privilege

– that I never questioned

ex.

Okay so, to explain, same day I walk out of work – after creeping along the road home

I am back at the boat we live in, deep breath before I board

(I get seasick sometimes but I never confessed to that properly)

I get down the steps through the blue hatch, and . . .

there he is

perched, sat on his cushion

playing his bass recorder

living his life.

I am

I'm stood – crouched, of course (I am tall, this boat was never gonna be big enough for me)

and as I tell the story of what happened I just need a hug, or something

I just need a *what? are you kidding?* or something

I just need a *you did the right thing* or something

or *that's kinda racist, yes*

and as I tell him what's happened

he's looking up at me

with his good listening face I-am-taking-in-what-you've-said

face

and he's getting up

he's taking my stuff, puts it down

I don't even know what happened, I just saw red

he's taken my hand in his

do we have any ice?

sits me down

he's kneeling in front of me

he cups his hands around my cheeks

and I just need an *ah fuck 'em* or something

solidarity, or something

and he says . . .

Violence is never the answer, babe.

. . . and that was the end of that.

Now, homeless

desperate

I find myself at this new door

the answer to a card on the board in Tescos one week
before

spare room, females only to apply, non-smoker, tidiness is
important, to live with mature woman

and even though only one of those things is true about me

in desperation I called the number 0207.

It's funny how

friends

they're never really there when you need them

or maybe I'd overspent my *I'm unhappy* cards and had
slowly drained them all

and family – I'm the youngest of four

my siblings are very high academic achievers,

it's quite demoralising

I'm a qualified mess

mainly, cos I still don't know what I want to do in life

– unacceptable if you're the child of an immigrant

and it's actually shameful when you realise you're in your thirties and single, again

and friends sit in their couple's nests happily yelling *you like to choose wrong*

again

or they yell *you walked out of another job?!*

again

yeah but I've been applying like crazy for jobs and I'll find something!

(I obviously didn't tell them what happened, either)

or my best mate decrees, with her chubby baby looking proper cute in her lap

aw mate, I'm so sorry, but honestly, honestly, I never got a good feeling about him!

– cheers, mate, thanks for the heads up before! yeah, hindsight is a wonderful thing

(*and for that horrible response I hope that your next nappy change is wrestling with shit that's so explosive, it's gone all the way up his back to his neck, you looseeeeeerr*)

too much?

I laugh, giggle about it, but inside I feel judged by everyone, a joke as I use up all my down-and-out cards

I sleep on settees

on floors

I own a sleeping bag

the tent I lost in the relationship purge.

Note to self –

in a break-up, when asked about your stuff, *where should I send that?*

never say *just throw it in the bin I don't want it*

and I certainly don't want to see you again to get it back

never say that

just go round and pick your stuff up

split up the records, plants, bedding

otherwise

you'll end up with a suitcase half filled with afro hair products

(too expensive to leave)

four loud shirts, and two pairs of jeggings.

Homeless (ashamed), I find myself at this door on the fifteenth floor

Mildred sounded okay on the phone

Mrs T to her face but

Mildred

elderly

Jamaican

who knows how this will play out, this could be the worst
idea I ever had but the room's cheap

and

until I find who I am

I won't go back home for more *grow up! and what about
doing a PGCE?* chat.

I won't call another mate to ask if I can crash

and

I'm gonna use this time to get myself together.

The mat below my feet says

welcome

(*well . . . thank you*)

I knock

can hear noises from the flats on the floor

above

below

it's a little

claustrophobic

and the mat's a little

traditional?

I turn to walk out of here

I feel sick

defeated

I feel like a kid hiding in a woman's skin

what a stupid idea

I'm walking away

when

I hear what sounds like eight different locks and bolts.

Mildred has opened the door behind me

afternoon, is all I hear

a low register

a singing voice

and I could keep walking, I could – I could walk away but
something in the voice makes me turn, for a second

hello, hi

she's half my height

looking me up and down

and her expression splits, she blinks, startled? like she's seen
a ghost, or something, but then she's caught herself and has
relaxed slightly

as I do that thing where I make my body half its height,
shrunk so I don't impose or scare . . .

we spoke on the phone earlier? that was me . . .

hmmmmph.

It's shoes off at the door, placed on the rack and through a
corridor,

weirdly without any photographs

in old people's homes they always have a ton of pictures,
right?

Mildred's a big woman

in the way some mature women get

gloriously

her skin's still spotless

and I wonder how old she is

this woman could have made it to her nineties already?
hard to tell

her wig's nice

flamboyant, even

I wonder how much hair she has underneath

if it's all grey

and what she thinks of me

I'm wearing three shades of green and when I catch myself
in the hallway mirror I realise I look

ridiculous

– I try to dress for my mood

or the mood I aspire to be and this somehow passed the test

this morning

and it was the only clean clothes I had

I'd ran out of clean underwear so have my swimming
costume on underneath

– felt like a reasonably acceptable idea at the time

so . . .

I'm sat on Mildred's patterned brown sofa

feel the plastic under my bum

and the glass of iced water in my hand which drifts to the coaster next to me

TV has been switched off

looks vintage, cute

a doorway with beads swung to one side leads to the kitchen, with a huge dutch pot

– so big it could cook me inside it – sat on the stove

something's brewing

smells good

smells so good – I'm hungry . . .

I can smell my childhood,

as I'm handed a laminated card with

house rules . . . ?

I'm grinning because I almost expect to see a curfew time at the bottom of it

but instead

if you drop it . . . pick it up

if you sleep on it . . . make it

if you open it . . . close it

I smile because I've seen this sign many times, but not since I was a kid

my own grandma's house

(we're separated by oceans – our family is spread out like most, across the globe)

so the memory of this sign

the memory, is

odd

I had problems

problems with the last tenant

Mildred sits opposite me and looks me square in the eye

and I am eight years old again

will I have problems with you?

no ma'am

noooooo. No. No problems. I am starting a new job,
tomorrow. You will get the rent on time. I am very reliable,
you won't even hear a peep out of me. Not. A. Peep.

Mildred doesn't quite know what to say

but it's obvious to me she doesn't want me here – as much
as I'd prefer to be able to

afford to live alone

in London

how awkward

she stares into my eyes for a second, holds me there

nods

and suddenly she appears sad

goes into the kitchen and so I head to my new room

brown walls

my single bed

my sad little suitcase

my plant

heating's on at least

and at least I'm safe

I've got to make this work, it won't be forever

got to make this last until I get myself together

got to get myself together

got to

And

I lie down, not thinking about my ex at all, what he's up to or whether he's wearing all my clothes whilst choking on the tears of his own grief.

In the same moment, five hundred and sixty-eight miles away

A teenager, a Muslim, is walking down his high street holding a sign.

This spot's as good as any, he thinks. It's busy, with shoppers passing by.

He places the sign in front of him. Stands back, and blindfolds himself with a piece of cloth and just waits.

The sign reads

I am not your enemy

hug me

and in between the lines you could read for yourself

I am sick

sick of the way people look at me
sick of the way I look at myself.

An older man passing stops, points.
Calls out to the teenager 'I'm coming in, okay?!'

2.

Alarm sounds

I have to set about fourteen of them just to get up

shower

lukewarm

punishment for crimes unknown

news on the smartphone

it's always bad, isn't it?

there's always something pretty messed up happening

someone dumb saying something stupid

or someone thinking they're woke being taken down

someone gross enough to touch someone where they really
didn't need to

and of course the usual blaming of immigrants

and a landslide

and I think what am I being distracted from?

sometimes the news is so bad that it overwhelms me

I want to vomit disgust in some moments and be still in
shock in others

news regularly brings me to tears

not just the bad news

– the good

the man who hasn't seen his mother in years and breaks down when she appears from the kitchen

security platform footage showing a rugby tackle right before someone attempts to jump in front of a train

kittens being saved from a roof (how'd they get up there . . .?!)

anytime I see someone Brown on the news saying

we need to take back control of our borders and immigrants I yell

SHAME

and throw something at the TV

I creep down the corridor past Mildred's room where I can hear

a thousand snorers snoring

out through the front door until it clicks

shut.

Coffee

tastes so, so

good – even if my smiling and flirting and looking directly in the eye hasn't landed me a freebie, dammit.

I move through the heat of rush hour

or as I like to call it, the passage of every-man-for-himself – *and-would-you-move-down-the-freakin-carriage-guys?!*

for me, it's a mixture of bus and tube pre-school run to get into town and a collective groan exhaled on the underground when the tube's late because of

someone under the tracks

a collective groan – have you ever witnessed that?

do people understand what under the tracks actually means?

people are so selfish.

This is a new day. A new day. And a new job.

I was worried I'd be blacklisted (weird word now I think about it) after the photoshoot freakout, but biscuit bossman sent an email saying as long as I signed an NDA stating I wouldn't tell anyone about my 'problems' with the office environment – and furthermore, if anyone asked, I'd had an exemplary time working there – they wouldn't press charges.

Felt fair to me.

So after a month of painfully applying for anything and everything, again

I am pretty nervous, today

I am just praying that I can keep my mouth shut in this new environment that I'm assuming will be

pretty much like the last one – only this time I'm gonna be quiet, like

undercover quiet, like, yeah so I need this job so I promise I'm gonna

fit in

fit in, fit in, don't stand out fit in

that's what I'm whispering to myself as I follow my new boss through the main entrance, look up and see floors of glass walls and someone slaps someone's ass slyly thinking no one saw it, she smiles back, and I'm like, wow, is that shit still happening now? And my new supervisor is pointing out the different rooms, walking quite fast, I'm struggling to keep up, take everything in, and he goes into the circular rotating glass door pod thingy and I follow him, and yeah it's tight in here but I realise too late – as he says

no, this is only meant for one person!!

only I've squished myself in already and

the shame

I don't know how to reply, he's gone so red and we have to wait until we squish round the other side before we're both free of each other's

breath.

It's not a good start

for this new day.

New day, new start.

I wonder what Mildred's up to, right now.

I'm sat at my new desk

– again, it's one cubicle of many

not really sure what to call what I do

I just kind of do what people tell me to

includes emailing, phone ringing, corporate computer buzzing and

oh god it's slow again

is yours slow?

server's slow again
server's down, everyone
eavesdropping is as much a part of our day as the work
dating and men and women and
hair
business, market
instagram
mortgages
unsubtle flirting and which sale you got that shirt in
power dressing is it?
stiletto heels, urgh
I'm just gonna keep to myself
you see I'm not here to climb up
this isn't part of the plan
phone beeps
server's crappy today
and then like that a day can be over.

The one good thing here, is Kemi
Kemi whose desk's next to mine
how she presents herself is meticulously outrageous
nails are all different colours
there's multiple styles of twists in her hair
and many different beads.

The first time we're introduced,

she's being asked to email something over *stat* and she replies

when I get to it, I'll do that.

I'm astonished – (when I get to it . . . when I get. To it. Wow.)

I pass her a Post-it with 'First day overshare, but I'm glad I'm sat here next to you. Cos, y'know . . .'

she passes one back saying 'You're funny! Definite OVERSHARE. LOL. Welcome. DFTBA'

dftba what does that even mean? Shame. Must be something good? So I reply

MTFBWY – may the force be with you. And she looks confused.

I am inspired by her Gen-Z no-bullshit what-I-do-is-not-up-to-you and I'll-wear-my-hair-how-I-want-to aura, immediately.

and I make a solid decision that one day I will be. her. friend.

and I understand that yes, I will definitely have to prove myself.

Right now Kemi is peering over the cardboard segmented between our units

this girl makes me giggle

I felt like wearing all my necklaces today

she decrees, and sure enough as she stands, I can't keep count

It's like a protest against all the chiffon, high heels, immaculate nails and pert smiles bouncing round this place

it's like an I-will-stand-out-if-I-choose-to-round-this-place

Nothing I could reply with would be cool enough so I
announce

OVERSHARE, and we giggle, me louder then her.

I wonder what she thinks of me.

I feel dull, next to her, bit of a nerd

I feel old in her presence

white in her presence

I am most definitely mixed in her presence

feel like I've neglected my roots

In her presence

she's effortless

beautiful

I'm busy trying to evaporate while

this woman does everything – even in this corporate
hellhole – on her own terms.

I bet Mildred would like her. Better than me.

There's a window nearby

a chunk of light

and if you stand by that window and look down there's
another office across the road full of these

creative people

I think they must be designers, they look cool with these funky spaceship chairs, basic clothes somehow styled to look like they're in the year 2056

there's neon and pink

and black

and they seem to drink coffee every second of the day

and move desks

and throw balls

sometimes one of them plays the guitar

one cycles into the room and the others laugh

sometimes they draw on the wall, in a good way

It's worth pointing out too that there's only one Black person in their office

that's one less than ours

but it looks like fun

I want to live in the space they inhabit.

What's your star sign? Date of birth? Time you were born?

Kemi says

okay so I've got this friend, yeah.

he's kinda alternative, like you

(what does that mean?)

so . . . can I set you up? He's really clever, he makes books. About insects

That's very sweet of her to worry for my emotional needs, but

not really my thing . . .

don't want to meet the love of your

fine she says

sticks her headphones in.

I think I've disappointed her –

she's at that age where she's still so,

and weirdly together

(*I want to live in the world you inhabit*)

In the same moment, three hundred and sixty miles away

An older woman on a bus can hear forced words. And then shouting. Because someone is being harassed a few seats down. The woman thinks will no one else speak up? Will no one else do it? The shouting turns from vulgar words to something ugly. The woman thinks I'm old. What if they turn on me? And her blood boils till the words come out

if you don't have anything nice to say to them, then shut the eff up!

silence

And she hopes, hopes that the drunken idiots aren't going to turn on her next, please!

3

At Mildred's

I'm trying to be a good tenant

I'm giving her space, I stick to my room, and to prove I can
be reasonably tidy, I'm hunting, for the – thingy

for the – hoover thing with the special bit that hooks on –
y'know, the other bit

my hand stretches up to the top shelf in the cupboard, and,
and thick wads of paper fall down by accident and as I
gather them up I'm holding these pamphlets, zines? worn,
handmade some of them

'Namibian Women Fight for Freedom'

manifestos

cool

and I hear Mildred's feet behind me as I go

they just fell down, sorry. These are really cool

Mildred casually goes *mmmhmmm* and grabs them from
me and goes into her room

(did I really need to call them cool?)

they're obviously on the ever growing don't-touch list

people don't even say cool, any more! Do they? Cool.

I cook

recipe led but then I get brave

Mildred's been pretending not to watch

but she definitely is, and this is definitely a

test!

she declines to try any (thank goodness)

because I don't know how to describe what I've made or
how I've wasted this food

 – I do a really bad job of pretending it's tasty and I am a
brilliant chef

but she's disappointed, I know it

and I am in no doubt I've

shamed my ancestry

as I run to Tescos for their premier scotch egg and avoid her
when back at the flat.

She's playing Betty Harris in the kitchen

I retire to my room

deflated

I'm curled up on my bed imagining that I'm being spooned

only I'm the big spoon

the space between where I want to be and where I am, is

deafening.

The bedroom door's being knocked

It's Friday night she says

excuse me?

Friday night she repeats

I come out from behind the door

I'd been curled up thinking about how I'll never have sex
again when she knocked

Friday – shouldn't you be out

dancing or something

with people yu age?

thanks so much I reply

but dancing?

noooooooooo

nope I'm going through the seven stages of grief

and I'm only in stage two

but no worries

no one's died – I'm just in mourning for my state of mind.

In this moment

I've definitely overshared

Mildred's looking uneasy

I think she might have heard me crying the night before and
I'm a little ashamed

when I say a little

I mean, a lot

It's okay, I'm conditioning myself to heal

*I'm gonna be just fine alone and I'm actually grieving for
the person I want to be*

this sounds even weirder

I'm about to start talking about myself in third person

Mildred's looking at me and
a man do dis?

Well not a man,
I now call him swampman – but actually it's more than that
kind of me swimming in a swampy pond. Of life
she's silent
I expect a hug
instead I get a sharp grab of my left arm and
put your shoes on

I wait for her in the corridor

wondering where she's going to take me

my imagination gets the better of me, from

Mildred's a secret millionaire she's sending me to an
expensive counsellor

to

Mildred's got a gun and she's going to shoot the ex and
biscuit bossman in the kneecap

not sure which I'd prefer, they're neck and neck

the stairs take ages for her to get down

stupidly I've not wondered since I've met her how she
makes the journey

or enquired after her health and the left leg she's a little
unsteady on

the journey takes an age

and by the end I've never been more grateful for my youth
or for my two good legs.

Down at the bottom
we shuffle outside and I creep beside her
we walk down the high street together
first time I've walked with an old person in years
the walk's so slow I can drink in the feeling of the road
I have time to look up
take in the tops of the cafes
the Black hair shops (memories sprout of scalp singes and
begging for them to wash the relaxer out of my hair – I
shudder)
arguments outside the betters
the woman selling the *Big Issue*
the guy in the wheelchair by the 242 bus stop, waiting for
the ramp to outstretch so he can board
it's taking its time as it beeps
someone's playing sax
and next to him, there's a homeless guy sitting by the
cashpoint – Mildred nods, asks after his sister as we pass,
sister's doing okay, yeh
while the new-build youth glide past in sexy trainers and
spaceship material

we're down a lane
stop outside an old pub that has somehow missed the

gentrification of this city

carpets are muddy

tables sticky

you can still smell the smoke on the furniture from when
we lit up indoors

Mildred orders two pints

screws up her face when told the price

I offer but

(*no*)

we sit down.

I open my mouth to say

this is (nice)

thanks for (the beer)

or maybe this is the perfect moment to say

I mean, I could confess

to this unsurmountable

loneliness

but I'm so ashamed

and so

we sit in silence for our pint

observing the empty bar

necking the beer

listening to the ska on in the background

silent

and I'm glad for it.

In the morning

I can hear the singing of the Pentecostals across the road

my eyes are forced open

**In the same moment, two hundred and eighty-three miles
away**

Cameras are pointed at an MP in a broadcasting studio.

**What she's just said will cost her – online bullying and
anonymous go-back-to-where-you-came-froms but the MP
is smiling because she wants to look strong.**

**But the newsreader sees a flash of pain behind her eyes, so
she turns to the camera and says *these people are cowards.
and they can get to. get to. you know where. thanks for
joining us.***

**The MP blinks, the man operating the camera gives a
thumbs-up to the newsreader, as a producer sprints down
the winding stairs towards them swearing their fucking guts
out.**

4.

The inhabitants of this building

make the walls sing, with different notes and rhythms, together

I hear different languages, and patois and

most people look each other in the eye

which I notice stops when we get outside

as the suspicion of strangers consumes us

– maybe the daily cycle of bad news dictates us to be afraid of the other

but inside here the walls breathe

that makes sense, they have been here a while, not like the matchstick new-build

not like me

some people have lived here for more than a few decades

the cement is heavy with exchanges and loves and pains and yells and laughs, and newborn cries and secrets and

and, I now realise that I never had my eyes open in the last places I'd lived

we were always in the cheapest place we could rent and I

never knew the names of my neighbours

never asked

but here

even though there's some suspicion with some

I'm learning

every time I leave the door on the fifteenth floor

learning the faces

a couple names I repeat over and over in my head after I've heard it so I never feel embarrassed to ask again

Gloria – who has her grandkids every weekend

Gloria

Samson – who has the tiniest dog even though he's the biggest guy

Samson

Tamika – hates but loves her fella who turns up every other week

Tamika

Stacey – one of her kids screams all the time

Stacey-with-the-kids Stacey.

Even though Mildred and I are

trying . . .

I'm pretty sure she thinks I'm annoying

not because I'm being rude, or anything, it's just.

she likes things a certain way

plates washed and stacked a certain way

no using the washing machine on a Sunday

a growing list of things not to touch

windows open at specific times

– which is fine, I'm just trying my hardest to learn how she
does it

and I'd like to say that my cooking has gotten better since
I've moved here

but I'd be lying

(I was taught via the watch-me-do-it class and it never
stuck)

Mildred's duckanoo is the best

'bluedrawers' I knew it by

one night I can't sleep, I open the fridge, mooching about
the shelves, and it's just there, waiting for me, calling to me,
so I take it out, I just set it on the kitchen surface, just for a
second, it said I should, so next I smell it, yep, I can tell it's
good. yeah. It's fresh. It's sweet. I unwrap a leaf. just
because. and I reckon a tiny bite can't hurt and if I cut a
sliver off she'll never know right and she's sleeping anyway
and next thing I know it's in my mouth and delightful and I
do a kitchen glory dance and of course she's suddenly there
standing, watching me, has caught me stealing, fork in
mouth, I try to style it out *the bit on the side looked odd so
I thought I should try it* and the lie is so bad.

it just tastes so so good..

I find out in time, I don't know half as much about the
world as Mildred.

and she likes to remind me of it.

Like when I come home with shopping and she enquires
where I got these *small small bags* of rice –

from the organic shop on the corner, I answer

and she belly laughs at me

all night

I'm annoyed because yeah I get it but I don't need a huge
sack of rice

she makes me tell her how much I've paid for everything in
my shopping bag and with each answer she laughs more

I feel like a dumbass gentrifier – which feels wrong because
can I even be that if I'm Brown and skint?!

of course I can.

Great.

Mildred likes every drink with ice

she goes to church on a Sunday and grumbles that the vicar
is too lenient –

he allows so-and-so to take over the service

she loves the market

feels every single avocado to make sure it's ripe, drives the
vendors mad

throws a hex when the price of breadfruits gone up, again

asks before she buys any grapes if *it's sweet yet?*

Mildred knows everyone she passes

and everyone knows her

as she strolls up the road she's always asking after so-and-
so's kid, or cousin

I see grown men fix up as she approaches them, it's quite
cool

the Turkish woman in the corner shop refers to her as Mum

which I like
Mrs T has weight in the area
and she knows it!

Watching Mildred watch telly is my favourite thing
she comments on EVERYTHING
when Diane Abbott addresses the commons she yells *preach*
when the Tories chat on *Question Time* she yells *lies*
or
rooting for the inferior animal *gwan!* when Attenborough is on
watching Mildred watch *EastEnders*
listening to her laugh
calling out
who's a badman
who's facety
most of the time she kisses her teeth and grimaces
these people . . .
de pickney dem . . .
but once, she clapped at the end of an episode
it had moved her, especially.

Dare I say it
I like being in her company
even if she takes the piss out of me

even if she's asked a couple times what I'm doing with my hair

not every day can look like a wash day, Mrs T

Tells her I'm good with how it is thanks

I like being in her company

even when she asks why I don't wrap my head before bed

or why I don't use a flannel

even if she likes to point out that

my legs look dry

give me strength! Mrs T. Too far.

But can I borrow some of your cocoa butter? I've ran out..

She stops going into my room to open the window

she only has to mention a few more times that my food needs

more seasoning before adding a heap to it

she belly laughs

I belly laugh

and

Mildred's green-fingered, too

she recognised that when I moved in my plant was in fact

a tiny mango tree

and her pride soars when I announce that I grew it myself, from a seed

I was sure I had proven my Blackness

as she pipes up

Can I have it?

No, Mrs T. No you can't.

I manage to get out of her that she was a youth worker for years

but now volunteers for the soup kitchen or hangs around at the women's refuge

gossips and provides unofficial advice

She's itchy when I ask her about Jamaica

will only say that she arrived in England in 1962

but her teaching qualifications didn't mean anything here

so she worked as a porter in a hospital

but when I press her for more –

oh, so what was that like? Back in the day?

Mildred turns the TV up.

I get the feeling she'd rather not talk about home

I mean her old home, is it even home any more?

or what it felt like when she first moved here

or

she doesn't have any family

I ask if she's always lived alone and she shrugs

and it feels like a sore wound – or maybe that's just what I'm putting on it

cos sure she gets around fine and has friends, and

y'know, she's very independent, yeah

but

y'know.

I begin to pop into the soup kitchen when she goes, begin to help out, she starts me off as chief pot-washer, until I'm able to prove myself

we do Friday film nights with salted popcorn

it feels

like a (home)

like I walked into this place for a reason

to be

here

because in time, I start to feel (present)

Present meaning comfortable in this new area. In hearing about old people's aches. Through eyes that aren't mine. Older eyes. Older skin.

She gives advice, freely, unasked for

like when I mention the swampman in passing, she answers

nuh expect nuttin fram a pig but ah grunt

erm, alright, Mrs T. Strong words. I like them.

or *stand up straight when your boss is talking to you, then he'll know who he's dealing with*

And it's good to hear this, and I reminder that anything I'm going through, it's nothing compared to what she had to deal with

So my confidence is slowly rising

as I accept in my new job, how to say

actually, I'm on my break right now. But erm, maybe can I give you a buzz when I'm done?

Or

I don't think so. Is that okay . . .? – bear with me here, I'm trying

I learn to ignore the things around me that I can't control

Like the office chat about how much drugs they got in on the weekend when all I can think about is who really pays a price for that?

I can kinda ignore that, but the news...

the every day of Brown humans named illegal

demonisation of our elders

Brexit

it's a blow,

genuinely upsets my spirit

and the struggle I have that I'm a part of this

system

It has a hold over me – something's not right

that's what I think about

pen in my mouth, at work, pretending to type.

In the same moment, two hundred and forty-three miles away

The post office queue is longer than usual. And a woman in the queues shattered, but a glance behind, and the stranger

beside her is having trouble standing. She doesn't want to ask him – *are you okay*, doesn't want to embarrass him, maybe he's fine. But as they wind their way to the front of the queue – it's her next and she turns to him and whispers

do you need to go ahead?

he jumps from the sound of someone addressing him.

Time to save face

she takes a step back for him to pass

you in a rush?

5.

Kemi has an offer to help spruce me up
so she puts it
which is how I find myself now
sat opposite
one of the hottest guys I've ever met
I'm gazing into his eyes, he has the most beautiful locs
and a really good grin.

I'm wearing a thong and it's really
uncomfortable
think I've put on some weight since I bought it as a
Let's-revive-our-sex-lives gift to the swampman
and now it feels like I'm wearing a tight
elastic band
across my vagina

we're chatting, with me trying to be as
minimally abusive to myself as possible
no taking the mick out of myself tonight
no over-talking
oversharing

and I don't think he spots me checking out our waitress
she's gorgeous!
Oh, he's cracked a joke ha – he's funny
he is funny
and, hang on,
I think he thinks I'm funny, too,
that's cool
(but)
don't mess this up now
(I dunno, what if)
nope, stop overthinking
I deserve this nookie in front of me, smile
so tell me about . . .
oh yeah?
no stories tonight about losing my mind at work
I hope he doesn't also live with an old person
or else we'll be finding a park
later
the chat's good
and no I don't get all his musical references but I pretend to
he doesn't order for me, tell me what I want to eat
doesn't interrupt me – in fact I'm just interrupting him!
sorry, sorry no I cut you off, go on
just the right amount of compliments so I don't feel
objectified
yessssssss

don't mess this up now

(I dunno, what if)

nope, stop overthinking

oh, he's five minutes into a paragraph

and it's obvious now

he knows I haven't been listening

not properly

literally no idea what he's just said because I've been trying to tell myself

not to mess this up or reveal too much or

(is there food in my teeth?)

Hang on

Oh yes he's flirting!

I think I'm flirting, the planets are aligned!

the sexy-time planets!

all the signs are right!

the planets are aligned, but

Big smile!

the planets are aligned, but

Big grin

the planets are aligned, but

I find myself thanking him

haven't enjoyed myself like this for a while
but actually

actually

I've got to head home

yeah, got to work

in the morning

(what am I doing?

what am I doing with this

opportunity

this moment this

hang on what am I doing?)

I've had a really nice night

Stop it

Well, yeah . . . work.

stop saying work

work, yeah

as I know I'm not gonna call him again

as I know I'm not ready to go through the good times to
bad times again

you see

I want to – I really want to but

how can I explain

I'm afraid of the skin I'm in

afraid of the skin he sees?

what everyone sees

I don't feel quite healed yet, fully present yet

so . . .

argh

I slump home

in one of those maddening questioning-myself slumps

being-hard-on-myself slumps

and it doesn't help that

Mildred's disappointed when the key hits the lock

she had high hopes for me tonight

maybe she was hoping I'd be moving out soon if it went well

stop it

how you back so early?

and I

filled with little food

along with too much wine

I feel a slight resentment suddenly

for the degree at which we are comfortable

because comfortable feels wrong, right now

I don't want to talk about it, I'm fine

she follows me into the kitchen as I neck a pint of water

what happen?

nothing, nothing, I'm fine, what've you got on TV?

as I plant myself on the sofa

she stares at me

what you doing back here?

I can feel my barriers wedging up

barricading

because this feels too familiar

feels like friend comfortable

family comfortable

the kind you don't want to hear

comfortable

and if I wanted family comfortable

if I wanted Black woman family advice I'd go home for that thank you

there was nothing wrong, we ate, that's it, it's fine, I just wasn't into it, is all – can we just watch a film or something? I'd like that

Mildred's stood in front of me, blocking the screen

why not?

she's not stopping

why's she not stopping?

let's just leave it at that

I sprint into my room to change into my pyjamas and then I'm back to the sofa

to a pair of unimpressed eyes

a pair of I-can-tell-you're-happy-sat-here-but-maybe-you've-got-a-little-too-comfortable eyes

you can't move on she says

need to step forward, you're holding yourself back

she's sat right beside me now

why's she not stopping? still not stopping, daring me to admit it

but I'm not going to

not going to say it

not going to

I'm sad!

I yell

I think I'm sad

and I tense up

I know you don't want to hear this, but Black people don't deal well with

sadness

I yell louder than I thought was coming out

maybe that's because your generation had to deal with all sorts of sadness

I don't know

but I do know that

Black people don't deal well

and don't lecture me, you're not exactly open yourself

I don't press you about your stuff

you have stuff!

like, so I reckon that you obviously haven't dealt well with grief

did I just said the word 'grief'? did I just say that? no

No

I don't think I did . . .
oh no I think I did

Mildred's skin's inflamed
nerves singed –
how yu chat about Black people?
what yu know about Black people?
I think you've shun yourself
shun who you are
and
you don't wear nice clothes so no one can see your beauty
while I yell back
that's SEXIST
I'm busy not conforming to gender stereotypes
living my life freely
Mildred kisses her teeth
the longest kiss in the history of teeth-kissing
well you can't hide from it all by sitting here with me she
says
you have to face it
you know what your problem is?
(*No but I'm sure you're going to tell me*)
you're not connected
she says
none of the youth are

you think you are

with your gadgets

but what do you even believe in?

you think you're sad?

there was a boy shot down the road

last week

bet you don't even know his name

you think you're sad?

they're deporting us, every week, and yu think you've done enough because you sign some petition, you come into this area and buy from the fancy shops, work in yu fancy office in town even though yu don't know what you want to do with your life, yu have no idea what we fought for when we came here

you kids

you, have no connection.

Her words have hurt me

deeply

I've always harboured a worry I was outside my (this) community and now

this

this hurts

so badly

so I attack back with

what connection?

how about where's all your pictures?
that says no reminders to me
no connections to me
and I might be living like this right now, with you
but I don't
intend
to spend the rest of my life without anyone
I won't end up alone
like you
renting my room out to strangers
how fucked up is that?!

the force of these words
my rudeness
hits the air so so hard

in the silence that follows
the floor seems closer to my face than before
the walls have caved in I'm sure
Mildred
leaves the room
I have overstepped, messed up
so badly
and she's right

I am not meeting my basic need as a human to connect
and her lack of faces in frames is none of my business.

In the same moment, a hundred and thirty-two miles away

The class is full, there's fifteen of them, and all together
they raise their hands and sign *how are you* for the first
time. Their first step learning this new language. BSL.
Practising *how are you, how are you*, smiles on faces, *me?
I'm fine, you good?* Strangers at desks with a common goal.

And there's one soul in particular, whose belly is giddy
thinking of how they will say *how are you* next week to
their new colleague.

6.

Why are hangovers worse as you get older? What's the
point in that?

Works unbearable if you're hanging.
thanks for the date Kemi, yeah, we will see
no nothing's wrong I'm fine

I'm miserable

what did I say to Mildred?

what exactly were the words I used?

Afternoon is a big meeting

there's maybe forty of us crammed into this tiny room,
we're all holding mugs of coffee and the chairman stands up

we're so sad to see her go, it's been a pleasure having you
work with us

and a woman smiles politely

the top's reorganising and she got pushed out

– when she heard

she threw a chair into the glass wall on the fifth floor

but annoyingly it didn't even crack, it stood firm

I need to point out that no one called security on her!

a guy started laughing

is she on her period ?

while two other women gossiped

does she know how long it's taken for us to get here?

and yes you're being pushed out but you can't show the pressure!

and now . . .

we're all in this meeting, cramped together

the chairman's speech is nearly over

thanks for being a part of our family

some dickhead starts to bring in a heavy slow clap, that doesn't quite catch on

thanks for having me

how do you even stand up in front of people when you've thrown a chair into a glass wall? I'm impressed actually.

I want to grab her as she leaves

grab her by the arm and say

I did that, yeah

I cracked too

but it was okay in the end

but instead I glance over to Kemi

and we share a let's-get-the-hell-out-of-this-place-before-it-eats-our-souls-alive

look

I remember the words I said last night

I won't end up alone

like you

but I probably will

I grab Kemi to own up to my bad behaviour

she listens intently until I'm finished

you've been a bit of a dick, yeah. but sounds like you're hurting. and sounds like she's hurting, too. And you look like you need some sugar or something, by the way

I show her my salad which looks like guinea-pig feed.

Kemi

gets out her Tupperware

crisps and cheese sandwiches chocolate Hobnobs cheesy puffs and a Freddo

holds her food up to the sky

it's like she's offering it to the gods

she holds her shit up there for at least twenty-five seconds

and then she brings it back down

I'm not sure what has just happened

was it a prayer?

I'm hungry
I'm thinking Kemi doesn't ever seem hard on herself
finds compassion for herself

when
my phone buzzes

Unknown number – I answer
it's a neighbour?
there's a lot of noise, yelling in the background
I can't hear really, but
something's happening with Mildred, I need to come home
line goes dead.

Stop.
jacket on
my supervisor is calling after me and
where does she think she's going as I rush past
emergency, sorry
I have to go
family
it splutters out without the sense that I've lied at all
before I've had the time to contemplate
the train couldn't have come fast enough
the bus either and I'm tapping my thigh

impatiently

surely, surely if it's an emergency then Gloria or someone should be there with her?!

The bus is in traffic, it's nearly at – practically at my stop, so to the driver

please can you open the doors, boss I plead

but he ignores me and so I do the only thing I can do in this situation, I pull the lever thingy like I've seen others do and nip out, fast as I can with the doors nearly licking me as I do it

I'm running to the top of our road

has she fallen over maybe?

taken a bath and can't get out?

I am racing like I've never ran before

I can see myself out of my body sprinting just to keep up with me

nearing heart arrhythmia

can start to make out a crowd, what the?!

crowd outside the main doors of our building, no

and oh my god

what did I say to her last night

the last thing I said I just hear over and over and over again

I won't end up alone

like you

like you

as I'm pushing through the crowd

people pushing back

let me through!

Mrs T?

Mrs T?

make my way through this forever circle

people MOVE need to get through and oh god is that her
shoe on the floor?

blood

can see her legs? no no no she is

Sat up.

the woman is fanning herself from a chair on the pavement

decadently

I rush up to her in disbelief

what's happened are you okay? are you alright?!

Mildred turns to me like a

Queen

I'm so sorry about gets clipped short

with a hug she gives me

a thousand years needed

and I am eight years old again

overwhelmed – she's okay – but *what happened*?

suddenly the police are coming up to us

while one yells to the crowd

*alright now everyone, let's move on, been nothing to see
here for a while now, move along now*

and Mildred whispers

look underneath mi bed

and with that

she's handcuffed?

the crowd jeer, people try to get in the way, they're arrested
too

one van's already full up with guys, another pulls up

Mildred gives me very dramatic don't-follow-me eyes as
she's whisked away

I'm so confused – what the hell has just happened?

One of my neighbours, Gloria's grandkid comes up to me

Mrs T man! Mrs T

she's bad y'know!

shows me a video on his phone – there's a group of posh
boys

it shouldn't matter that they're posh

but it does because they're behaving like pricks

taking the piss out of the homeless guy (one with the sister)
sat beside the cashpoint

these three wankers are drunk, even though it's still early,
really

and having a go at him

he gets up, yells something back

there's a stand-off and they're laughing, laughing at him

you can smell the

privilege

I feel like this is a metaphor for Boris, Michael and Nigel

but one of these three idiots is Black

and it shouldn't piss me off but it does

these three are bold

and who pushes the guy first it's hard to tell

but there's a kinda crowd gathering

so the three start telling people to piss off

and

enter

Mildred.

She comes into the frame

leave him alone

leave him

one guy's yelling *stay out of it you bitch, my business, is my business you*

and before he's had a chance to use the word 'bitch' again

whooooooooooosh

she's knocked him flying with her handbag

the camera pans round to the crowd, shouting along angles and

naaaaaaah man!

this kid's filming skills are incredible, he needs to get trained go to film school

or something

in fact

forget film school he's skilled!

the guy's down on the floor from the force of the bag hit

does she have a brick in there or something?

the other two run off but Mildred reaches one, she's moving faster than I've ever seen before

she's the female Black Yoda

whoooooosh

second guy's down too

and stunned

shame

Mildred turns to the crowd as they are calling out, she grins, they cheer,

and then in an unthought moment, high on the buzz

she does some kind of WWE wrestling jump on him

I shit you not

and the crowd go wild

the third posh kid comes back stupidly, he's got his hands up

but Mildred shows no mercy as she hits him on the hip with her bag with such a force I wonder if she represented Jamaica in the national shot-put team in her youth.

I hand the kid back his phone

there's a lot to take in

and I'm still recovering from my sprint here, but grinning
because even if I am a wannabe pacifist
that was great
and in the event of the zombie apocalypse
I'd want Mildred by my side
not for her brutal strength
but her strength in the face of injustice
and I need to find the homeless guy
find out his name
so I can stop calling him
homeless guy, like he's solely defined by that
and because without his name I am undoubtably
part of the problem.

As the crowd disperse I wonder if Mildred will become an
overnight YouTube sensation
and how much she enjoyed whupping those boys.

I crawl up to the fifteenth floor
the flat's so quiet, open the door to her bedroom
I look around for a second
at the frills on the curtains
patchwork quilt on the bed
a candle on the table
I crouch down, and reach my hand under her bed
there's more than a few

sheboxes to navigate

and I'm worried what my hand will touch

worried I'm going to find her vibrator

– not judging if she has one, but what if it's better than
mine?

the first two boxes I open

shoes

third

inside is an old photo album

I pick it up.

In this moment, fifty-six miles away

**Two daddies are holding their baby. It's their first night as a
family. They put the baby down slowly, into the cot. The
baby stirs, big yawn. But is fast asleep. The daddies look at
each other. Hold each other. High five.**

7.

The album's old

years old

my fingers peel the cover

and it's open, and

a young Mildred stands

smiling

It's a black-and-white photograph, it's the sixties

I can tell from her miniskirt (yeesh) and the handsome men
in hats

she's stood at Piccadilly Circus

one fist proudly up to the sky

some of the rest hold signs

Black Power

Equality

Liberation

Smash Fascism

Save the Trees

and there's a woman, of a similar age to Mildred, holding
her hand

a woman who weirdly looks –

Looks kind of like me? whispering something in her ear

or, is it a kiss?

they're holding hands, and Mildred's eyes are singing
we are together
and we're going to change the world

I'm stunned
these pictures
this Black joy
jubilance and strength spring out of each one
and, now something makes sense –
the way she looked at me the first time we met
the zines I found that she didn't want me look through
the walls without pictures
the past has hung, heavy
past's been hidden, buried, gone
and something tells me – I reckon these people, they're long gone, too.

On the final picture, is a faint inscription
'Remember. Connection is an act of rebellion.
With love always,
Sylvana'

A creak behind me confirms
Mildred's stood there
I've no idea how long I've been sitting

outstretched on her bedroom floor

it could have been hours, as

tears have rolled down my cheeks without my permission.

go fetch the rum in the cupboard

I get up, obediently.

We drink in silence

the TV is on low, news is on,

we're quiet, until I finally ask what happened at the police
station and *by the way*

you've got some badass moves

she chuckles – *one of the officers at the station, I've known
him since he was a boy . . . so . . .*

y'know . . . I know his mother, so . . .

I've still got the picture in my hand, which I hold up

Who's Sylvana?

Mildred looks at it a long time.

I lost her. long time ago. She passed, suddenly.

It was me, and her . . .

we carry on drinking

our rum and ginger beer

I manage *I'm sorry*

and she waves her hand

like that's all that needs to be said

but I'm ready, ready to try, ready to shed something – so

before I met you. I lost control.

I think I'd trained myself to take up as little space as
possible, until there was nothing left of me and so I broke,
and I've been struggling to connect, even now I'm afraid I'll
go about it the wrong way, like before. I've felt so so small.

She sighs,

I fought

we all did, for a long time

think I don't know what feeling small feel like?

angry at the world feel like?

This world can be brutal, especially for people like us. But
we have to try.

In between her words is unspoken utter grief.

I've been sat on the floor, she on the couch

and I feel a hand parting my hair

a comb pulling through

as I'm

holding the cream in my right hand

she's doing it gently

not the way I remember
only a slight pull on my unruly knots
as she takes her time
lovingly

It's perfect.
and then Mildred starts to chuckle
what? I ask, longing to be a part of the giggle
Mildred belly laughs
what? what!

*when we first spoke on the phone about the room, I
thought you were a white girl*

Cheers, Mrs T.
Way to ruin a perfectly beautiful moment.

In this moment, five miles away

**It's dinner time. Their son is hiding outside the door.
Hiding because he's wearing a skirt – it feels right. The son
walks into the kitchen, and sits. His mother stares.**

**And then squeals *where'd you get that from? You look
gorgeous.***

8.

I want to do something nice for Mildred.

I tell her we're going on a trip, and we hop on the 38 into town

she hasn't been into town in ages

can't remember the last time, avoids it

and as we pass through Islington and Clerkenwell she tells me

what every

other

shop used to be

a memory here

a thought across there

a kiss

she cusses out the driver loudly when he stops to regulate the service

It's the only kind of London tour I ever want to take.

I've asked Kemi to meet us

and she's there waiting as we get off the bus

Kemi is in a polka-dot top, jeans and a bright headscarf

bangles of every colour

Mildred is in a dark dress

I introduce her as my aunt

I introduce Kemi as my mate who I was working with (past tense implied as I intend to quit the job I hate!)

we're walking

although

pretty slowly

taking in town

Mildred's chatting about this and that

Kemi is asking questions about Jamaica, and when she got here,

Mildred's answering freely

which amuses me

she wants ice cream, which we buy

a busker, guitar in hand, sings some Joan Armatrading

and we are enjoying our capital like tourists, with new eyes,

and then

we get to it.

the destination I alone planned.

Piccadilly Circus.

Mildred stops

looks over to me, and then towards the monument.

She walks towards it

(I've been worried that this might upset her)

and I whisper to Kemi

I hope this is okay

Mildred stands at the edge.

It's busy, today, like always

the proper tourists are dotted about, taking photos

It's a little crowded and Kemi tells them

make way, people, elder coming through

as Mildred stretches to place her hands on the fountain

looks up towards the wings, the bow, the arrow

steps back down and circles it to find the exact spot she
stood with her girlfriend Sylvana in the picture

finds it

and stops

is unsteady as she climbs the steps once more

we look on

we look on, as

In this moment

five yards from me

skipping distance

there's an elderly woman

who has covered her face with a heavy hand

the shame of the weight of emotion

shame of being seen

shame of showing your true self

we look on as a tear crawls down

each cheek

and hear a heavy deep heave

which turns in a bigger noise

a cry

a bawl

not a Western human sound

I start to stutter *I'm sorry, sorry I didn't mean to –*

shall we go? it's okay

but she looks to me

her whole face wet

she looks at me and then

upwards

as pellets of water fall from the sky

it's raining. great, didn't bring the umbrella

think we need to move till it passes

she shakes her head

the rains becoming biblical

but she doesn't want to move, and sure enough the proper
tourists creep under umbrellas and run for the cover of the
shops across the junction

but Mildred's staying put

we're getting wet

and it sprays down on us

harder, heavier, the three of us alone now at the monument

I don't want you to catch a cold, I think we should

Mildred starts to laugh

oh dear

I think we should go

crack up

okay I'm actually starting to get worried, now

belly laugh

what?

crying with laughter

What?!

she raises her fist to the sky

an offering

holding it there

ten centimetres from me

Mildred is raising her fist to the sky

and then

she pulls her fist to her chest

beats her chest hard

one large thud

she beats her chest again

and again, slowly,

looks me in the eye, and I think, I think,

I think I understand

she's showing me how to do it, properly

I stop caring if anyone's watching us

or worry if I look ridiculous –

instead, I embrace this feeling

my hand finding my chest finding it's

rage

as

Mildred's fist has stretched into a wide palm

and she slaps her chest

hard

as I follow

we follow

Kemi's joined in

as we are pelted by the rain turned into

hail

hailing tiny chips of ice

in Piccadilly Circus

and this thud turned slap turned move in the hail turns into

three of us paying tribute to the shoulders before and the
act of together

the act of together

act of new skin honouring old skin

act of care

act of

I see you

And there isn't anywhere else I'd like to be. Anywhere else in the world, right now, in this moment. Than right here.

Mildred looks at me

nods

and then turns her face up to the sky

and

roars

and I

I

roar

too.

And ten yards from us, a little girl is staring at us roaring. And joyfully, she starts to wiggle